Democratic Genetic
ENGINEERING

Chauncey Chen

LifeRich Publishing is a registered trademark of The Reader's Digest Association, Inc.

LifeRich Publishing books may be ordered through booksellers or by contacting:

LifeRich Publishing
1663 Liberty Drive
Bloomington, IN 47403
www.liferichpublishing.com
1 (888) 238-8637

ISBN: 978-1-4897-1901-0 (sc)
ISBN: 978-1-4897-1912-6 (e)

Print information available on the last page.

LifeRich Publishing rev. date: 08/28/2018

TO THE BUILDERS OF A BETTER WORLD

CONTENTS

PREFACE

A Bleeding World

The common by-product of the world financial crisis, the Arab Spring, and the Occupy Wall Street movement is blood. There are political unrests in Egypt, Iran, and Turkey, especially the bloody civil war in Syria.

The Meaning of Freedom and Democracy

In 1999, I published a health book titled *Dynamic Chikung* (American Literary Press, Inc.). Assuming people might be more interested in health books, I included "A Project to Complete Democracy in the USA" in that book to arouse urgent attention to the issue, suggesting all sectors, no matter public or private, should establish their authorities by periodic democratic elections to eliminate "institutionalized bureaucracy" that seemed to be everywhere. I got no response.

Later, I sent letters to a number of billionaire celebrities who seemed to be interested in politics, suggesting they run for presidency in the hope that they could keep political independency by paying for their political campaigns by themselves. Again, I got no response.

Letter to President Clinton

In 2000, Al Gore—former US vice president—won the popular vote, but former governor of Texas George W. Bush won the presidency by winning the electorate vote. In January 2000, I wrote a letter to

President Bill Clinton to express my concerns about democracy in the United States.

1) Based on the fact that a president was selected by a 5–4 majority of the Supreme Court justices appointed by elected presidents, a nation's disputable votes were invalidated and even banned from further clarification. Is it democratic?
2) The American people are not allowed to vote for the president directly. They are only allowed to vote for the Electoral College electors who vote for the president. Is it democratic?
3) Is our government of the people, by the people, and for the people? Not exactly.
4) How do we reform, then? I suggested one word: democratization.

Democratic Genetic Engineering

President Clinton was the only person who replied with a letter encouraging me to get involved. Since then, more than fourteen years have passed. In these years, I did research and drafted numerous manuscripts that seemed satisfying but were discarded. The issue is complicated.

When the world financial crisis, Arab Spring, and Occupy Wall Street brought massive demonstrations, unrest, and violence almost everywhere—escalating into civil wars in Syria and likely in Egypt—people set themselves on fire to send messages and demand that their requests be fulfilled.

These are very familiar issues about democracy and freedom of speech since both are either established as fundamental laws in many constitutions or proclaimed in the United Nations Universal Declaration of Human Rights (UNUDHR, attached in the appendix) as well. Most member states signed this monumental document crystallizing the lessons learned from World War II when sixty million people were victimized. The UNUDHR has thirty articles that cover all aspects of human life in dignity and the brotherhood of man.

If we study these articles closely, we can see that if the ideas in these articles had been implemented well, the world might not be facing the crises it is facing today—and people would be living much better lives. Why wasn't the UNUDHR implemented for sixty-six years after its proclamation in 1948?

One of the reasons was that the United Nations did not have enough executive power to implement the UNUDHR while calling upon all UN member states to promote the text of the UNUDHR principally in schools and other educational institutions, without distinction based on the political status of countries or territories. This, however, could not explain why the member states that have signed the UNUDHR could not implement the UNUDHR by themselves. The evidence is that 1.29 billion people are living under the poverty line with a child dying every few seconds. Such wide deficiency could only be explained by fundamental flaws in the concept of democracy and freedom and its subsequent implementation. Let us see what is missing.

Direct Democracy

The earliest documented direct democracy was Athens, a city-state in ancient Greece where qualified voters could speak their minds, be heard, debate, and vote for legislature and its execution. Nowadays, even small towns are many times larger than Greek city-states. This direct democracy existed for only 128 years and was stopped mainly by Alexander the Great's invasion from Macedonia.

Contemporary Democracy

The size of modern cities makes it impossible to exercise direct democracy. Instead, we have representative democracy, which means voters do not exercise democracy directly as in Greek city-states. They elect representatives to do so for them. The problem is that while voters may know something about the issues, in general, they do not specifically know their candidates well. Most voters find it easy to watch television to learn something about the candidates they will elect or reject. This situation means that the more frequent the appearances of the candidates on television, the more chance for them to win.

Modern television presentations are ultraexpensive. Political candidates need a lot of money to finance their campaigns, and in fact, they spend a lot of time raising it. There are basically three types of political campaign financing: public financing, private financing, and a combination of both.

Deprivation of the Principle of Equality of Rights

No matter whether the campaign funding is public, private, or a combination of both, only a handful of people can have it or get it. This divides the voter population into two classes. Only few can speak out and be heard since only they can afford the ultraexpensive modern media; the vast majority of voters can speak but cannot be heard. This is the most severe deprivation of the majority of the fundamentals of democracy—the principle of equality of rights, opportunity, and treatment, which is the premise of both freedom and democracy.

The essence of democracy is that common people are the wielders of political power. In Athenian democracy, citizens expressed, communicated, and debated the premise that they could speak out, be heard, and be treated equally.

Contemporary democracy, however, only allows a few candidates to be heard on television sets. This booklet tracks what happened and could happen while the overwhelming majority does not have a say to be heard and respected. It proposes peaceful reform other than what is happening now in the world financial crisis, the Arab Spring, and the Occupy Wall Street movement. It is divided into six chapters; each of them addresses a key issue.

Chapter 1 briefs a suffering world in the world financial crisis, the Arab Spring, and the Occupy Wall Street movement. It also examines violent political unrest in many countries and how these mass movements need unified goals to succeed.

Chapter 2 points out the unified goal of the mass movements was established in the United Nations Universal Declaration of Human Rights (UNUDHR) in 1948. Then it checks critical articles of the UNUDHR against facts only to find this monumental document has not been implemented well for nearly seventy years.

Chapter 3 scrutinizes contemporary democracy and finds its conceptual flaws leading to the deprivation of a majority of voters of the principle of equality of rights, opportunity, and treatment of the people that is the basis of both freedom and democracy.

Chapter 4 proposes democratic genetic engineering (DGE) that requires freedom of information (FOI) be free of arbitrary interpretation and proposes free government political media (FGPM) for all and free speech forum (FSF) for private sectors.

Chapter 5 seeks cognitive truthfulness for the proposed FGPM and FSF, taking into consideration the discovery of quantum mechanics that the world is wave-particle dualistic. Opposites are natural and complementary. Opposition should be resolved by creative synthesis and brotherly constructive cooperation to attain peace, stability, and progress.

Chapter 6 suggests a systematic approach of targeted philanthropy will help common people move from struggling to making a living to enjoy living a human life, receiving education, doing research, choosing the work they love most to make unique contributions to the making of a better world by creativity and invention, and making the dream of universal brotherhood "one for all, all for one" come true.

NOTES

CHAPTER 1

DEMOCRATIC GENETIC ENGINEERING

A Suffering World

About 2,500 years ago, the Buddha said, "Life is suffering." It is true that life may suffer from many causes: physical pain, bad health, poverty, aging, depression, etc. Paradoxically, the realization that life is limited is most suffering of all.

No matter how painfully life suffers, most people prefer to live than to die. Yes, there are cases when people do not want to live anymore and have decided to die, and in fact, there are doctors who help people die even at the risk for offending laws, but it is rare.

"Life is a gift from God," religious people solemnly claim. For unreligious people, life itself has its supreme, intrinsic value. It means happiness—or the pursuit of happiness. Death, the ending of life, causes grave sorrow to close survivors and common sadness to the human mind.

Sadly, in the twenty-first century, about 2,500 years after the Buddha, our world is still suffering.

World Financial Crisis

Toward the end of 2008, the world started suffering from the most painful financial crisis since the Great Depression in the 1930s. It began with bad subprime mortgage loans in New York City and soon engulfed more banks and financial institutions in the US. It later spread to Europe and Asia, and it has now assumed global proportions through globalization.

People were stunned when capitalist icons collapsed, governments bailed out mortgage and banking giants for hundreds of billions, banks took over signature stockbrokers, and banks took over other banks.

The stock market plunged immediately, though with small rallies, it came back now and then via man-made stimulations. Worldwide, trillions were lost. Many manufacturing and departmental giants closed, partially closed, or were bailed out. An inevitable result was massive layoffs and home foreclosures. People who had been working for their entire lives lost their life savings—they could not retire as planned and had to work indefinitely. Protests were held in many big cities.

Humanity Suffers Most

It is hard to imagine how one feels when losing job and home simultaneously. A former California financial specialist found a simple solution: he shot his whole family and then himself. He was laid off and could not find a job for several months.

In the first months of 2009, similar family tragedies happened in Hong Kong on a weekly basis—whole families jumped from skyscrapers. In Japan, hundreds of thousands committed suicide. Surprisingly, even a German billionaire Adolf Merckle took his own life. Worldwide there are continuous families tragedies, suicides, and homicides, here or there, now or then. The civilized world was no longer a paradise in the twenty-first century. Billions of people lived in primitive conditions without clean drinking water.

Arab Spring

The world financial crisis has been causing an ever-worsening situation. On December 17, 2010, a twenty-six-year-old Tunisian fruit vendor

Mohamed Bouazizi (1984–2011) set himself on fire in protest of the confiscation of his wares and the harassment and humiliation inflicted on him. A female municipal official slapped his face, and her aides beat him. Later he was even denied a meeting with higher officials about complaint.

Bouazizi had been struggling to make a living to support his mother and siblings. He borrowed money to run a fruit business on a one-wheel cart, which usually didn't require permission. This, however, could be granted only after the officials had received sufficient bribery. Bouazizi was hardly able to make ends meet—not to mention bribing local officials for permission to work.

He set fire to himself, becoming a torch that lit up the dignity of the human soul in his area. The unspoken message was: *I would rather die with dignity than live in shame.*

People became extremely angry and frustrated. They assembled and risked their lives to support Bouazizi's act. Thus, the revolution began with demonstrations and riots throughout Tunisia in protest of political and social injustices in the country. The intensity of anger and violence compelled President Zine El Abidine Ben Ali to step down on January 14, 2011, after twenty-three years in power.

Following Bouazizi's example, in the Arab world, a number of self-immolations attempted to bring an end to the autocratic governments.

Inspired by the Tunisian revolution and the martyrs, the revolution spread to many other countries. The protesters used modern communication technology to communicate, and they raised awareness in the face of state attempts to repress protests and enforce Internet censorship. They organized civil resistance movements in sustained campaigns involving strikes, demonstrations, marches, and rallies that met violent responses from governments as well as from pro-government militias and counterdemonstrators. These attacks were answered with violence from protestors.

The young people of Egypt led an eighteen-day revolt that ousted President Hosni Mubarak on February 11, 2011, shattering three decades of political stasis and overturning the established order of Egypt. Mubarak is under arrest for investigation of corruption. On

May 23, 2012, the Egyptian people had a presidential election for the first time in five thousand years of civilization.

Unfortunately, developments in Egypt after the ousting of President Morsi on July 3, 2013, may lead Egypt to a civil war. A civil war in Libya resulted in a regime change and the death of its dictator, Gaddafi. Syria is fighting a bloody a civil war that started on June 12, 2012. Political unrest in protesting undemocratic regimes has spread to Turkey and other countries.

Occupy Wall Street (OWS)

The suffering continued. On September 17, 2011, demonstrators started an "Occupy Wall Street" (OWS) movement in Zuccotti Park in New York City's financial district. A Canadian activist group, Adbusters, who originally called for the protest, proposed peaceful occupation of Wall Street to protest social and economic inequality, legal injustice, corporate greed, and the influence of corporate money and lobbyists on government and democracy. They questioned the absence of legal repercussions for the bankers behind the global financial crisis, especially those who were responsible for the crisis. Instead, they actually received government bailouts, and some made even more money than before. The disparity in wealth grew absurdly and unfairly.

The OWS was inspired by Arab Spring protests such as those in Tahrir Square (January 17, 2011) in Cairo, England (November 2010), and Greece (April 2003). In June 2011, Spain held antiausterity protests of the *indignados* (indignants). Continuous protests were held in America, Europe, Asia, and other parts of the world as a result of the world financial crisis, and there were earlier protests against globalization at the G8 and G20 summits. The protests were promoted rapidly by social media (e-mail, Facebook, YouTube, Twitter, etc.).

The OWS movement spread to many cities with the key slogan: *We are the 99 percent. We are too many to fail.* They were close to the White House in October 2011. Worldwide, whether people were actually participating in occupying movements or just watching them, many agreed with this slogan. According to the Associated Press, on November 16, 2011, in Washington, DC, a band of super-rich people petitioned Capitol Hill to urge Congress to tax them more.

Different politicians cast the Wall Street protests in a very different light. No matter what they might label the movement, this event shows the human mind has a somewhat universal fairness scale, disregarding how rich or poor they are. In the final analysis, without such a universal scale, human society could hardly sustain itself.

Some criticism about the OWS movement is that the participants have not joined their forces together since they do not have a unified goal and a plan to reach that goal. Such a movement cannot sustain itself and is bound to fail.

When a mass campaign has no unified goal and plan, the participants tend to move in different directions that scatter efforts and energy until exhaustion and the movement dies out. On the other hand, it is equally true that if the participants do not have something in common, there cannot be a mass rally in the first place. The question is how well this common goal has been established.

Revolutions of this scale with such massive participation can only be ignited when many people suffer from unbearable living conditions. This includes insults of human dignity, aching poverty, desperately increasing unemployment, ever-rising inflation, and pitch-dark government corruption. Worst of all, people felt powerless to appeal or protest—not to mention correcting it. What to do? When human tolerance reaches a certain limit, burning red blood kindles a fire. This happened when Mohamed Bouazizi set himself on fire to protest the confiscation of his wares. This situation set an example to many followers who would rather die with honor than live in shame. Human beings, however, live only once. Apparently the line between life and death has faded for the "martyrs" in the Middle East, but it has not yet disappeared since most demonstrators still want to live—if not for themselves—for their loved ones. Whether they have decided to die or live, one task is common: showing the world what is on their minds.

It is very simple indeed. What they want to do is to send a message for their demands to be fulfilled. If so, why is it so difficult? Why did

Bouazizi have to burn himself to send out a message that was worth more than his life? Has not freedom of speech been written in the United Nations Universal Declaration of Human Rights (UNUDHR) and almost all democratic constitutions?

CHAPTER 2

UNITED NATIONS UNIVERSAL DECLARATION OF HUMAN RIGHTS

The United Nations Universal Declaration of Human Rights (UNUDHR) is a milestone document in human history. Drafted by representatives with different political, legal, and cultural backgrounds from all regions of the world, the UNUDHR was proclaimed by the United Nations General Assembly in Paris on December 10, 1948— General Assembly resolution 217 A (III)—as a common standard of achievements for all peoples and all nations. It sets out, for the first time, fundamental human rights to be universally protected.

A Brief History

During World War II, the Allies adopted the Four Freedoms—freedom of speech, freedom of assembly, freedom from fear, and freedom from want—as their basic war aims. The atrocities committed by Nazis taught the world community to reach the consensus that a universal declaration to specify the rights of individuals was necessary. In other words, the UNUDHR was written with the blood of the sixty million victims of World War II.

The United Nations human rights program has grown considerably since its modest beginnings some sixty years ago. Organizationally, it started as a small division at United Nations Headquarters in the 1940s. The division later moved to Geneva and was upgraded to the Centre for Human Rights in the 1980s. At the World Conference on Human Rights in 1993, the international community decided to establish a more robust human rights mandate with stronger institutional support.

The UN General Assembly on December 20, 1993, in the wake of the World Conference on Human Rights established the Office of the United Nations High Commissioner for Human Rights (OHCHR) that works to promote and protect the human rights that are guaranteed under international law and stipulated in the UNUDHR.

Drafted as "a common standard of achievement for all peoples and nations," the declaration set out basic civil, political, economic, social, and cultural rights that all human beings should enjoy for the first time in human history. Over time, it has been widely accepted as the fundamental norm of human rights that all governments should respect.

The UNUDHR, the International Covenant on Civil and Political Rights and its two optional protocols (December 16 1966), and the International Covenant on Economic, Social, and Cultural Rights (December 16 1966) form the International Bill of Human Rights.

http://www2.ohchr.org/english/law/

Following this historic act, the United Nations Assembly called upon all member countries to publicize the text of the UNUDHR and "to cause it to be disseminated, displayed, read and expounded principally in schools and other educational institutions, without distinction based on the political status of countries or territories."

UNUDHR and Human Life

The UNUDHR consists of thirty articles aimed to address all aspects of human life. According to the intent, effort, and expertise crystallized in the making of—and the hope cherished by all member states and humankind after the proclamation of the UNUDHR—we should live in a brotherly world with love that has rarely been enjoyed by civilization. In a world of brotherhood, violence is less likely to happen. Even if it did happen, it may be easier to resolve peacefully. Let us look at the UNUDHR more closely. The following are some critical articles:

Brotherhood (Article 1)

All human beings are born free and equal in dignity and rights. They are endowed with reason and conscience and should act toward one another in a spirit of brotherhood.

Facts

After the proclamation of the UNUDHR on December 10, 1948, many old wars continued. New wars broke out, such as anticolonialism and people's wars, coups, invasions, ethnic and religious conflicts, terrorism. Such wars did not show the spirit of "brotherhood" as solemnly stated in Article 1 but hostility and killing one another.

Now we see a bloody, hellish civil war in Syria and violent, bloody conflicts in Egypt and many other countries. In addition, the most dangerous product of the Cold War (superpower nuclear antagonism) started soon after World War II pushed humankind toward the edge of annihilation. The danger is still hanging on.

Slavery (Article 4)

No one shall be held in slavery of servitude; slavery trade shall be prohibited in all their forms.

Facts

Human trafficking and slavery in the twenty-first century is a multibillion-dollar business. Millions are enslaved in one form or another, and a slave can be bought for as little as a hundred dollars. CNN has started a program called "Freedom Project" to help stop slavery.

Inhuman Torture and Degrading Punishment (Article 5)

No one shall be subjected to torture or to cruel, inhuman, or degrading treatment or punishment.

Facts

Waterboarding has become a frequent torture technique; disregarding it is directly against this article.

Adequate Living Standard (Article 25)

(1) Everyone has the right to a standard of living adequate for the health and well-being of himself and of his family, including food, housing, and medical care and necessary services, and the right to security in the event of unemployment, sickness, disability, widowhood, old age, or other lack of livelihood in circumstances beyond his control.

(2) Motherhood and childhood are entitled to special care and assistance. All children, whether born in or out of wedlock, shall enjoy the same social protection.

Facts

Approximately 1.3 billion people are living on less than $1.25 a day, which is the world poverty line. Hundreds of millions do not have access to improved sources of drinking water, and more lack access to improved sanitation facilities.

According to the Food and Agriculture Organization (FAO) of the United Nations, more than one billion people are undernourished.

More than two billion suffer from a lack of essential vitamins and minerals in their food. Nearly six million children die every year from malnutrition or related diseases, which is about half of all preventable deaths.

Freedom of Opinion and Expression (Article 19)

Everyone has the right to freedom of opinion and expression; this right includes freedom to hold opinions without interference and to seek, receive, and impart information and ideas through any media and regardless of frontiers.

Facts

The continuous demonstrations against the G8 meetings, financial crisis, Arab Spring, and the Occupy Wall Street movement prove that "freedom of opinion and expression" does not work well, and the rights to such freedom are not protected. When the rights are not protected, people organize themselves to protect their rights through mass protests. In Libya and Syria, such protests have escalated to civil wars, bloodshed, and sacrificing human lives and the most basic human rights.

Key Issue

Human rights still suffer from many causes sixty-six years after the proclamation of the UNUDHR in 1948. No matter how complicated the causes are and how many excuses there are, nonbrotherhood is the key.

Who would allow brothers not to have clean water to drink, food to eat, and a home to live in? And worse, who would deny brothers the right to speak out? This is the core problem of contemporary democracy and freedom.

NOTES

CHAPTER 3

UNUDHR AND CONSTITUTIONS

Most member states of the United Nations have signed the UNUDHR in anticipation of a better world. The reality, however, is many violations of the UNUDHR led to worldwide demonstrations, unrest, bloody violence, and loss of innocent lives. Why?

The United Nations has no executive power to enforce the UNUDHR. This, however, cannot explain why many member states with similar constitutional articles on democracy and freedom of expression are poorly implementing their own constitutions and the UNUDHR they supported and signed. As a result, political unrest is happening in almost all member states as described above.

There are many basic types of government in our time that can be classified into three basic types:

- democratic
- undemocratic
- transitional

In the twenty-first century, democracy is the main political trend. After thousands of years of civilization, the human mind is awakening to recognize individuals' inherent equal and inalienable rights. Human beings demand to know and defend their human rights through their own struggles—even at the price of their lives. No force can stop this movement in any type of government. Sooner or later, it will become democratic—either through peaceful evolution or violent revolution since nothing can stop the awakening of the mind for a better world that the mind is created for. The collapse of the former Soviet Union in 1991 is powerful proof of this fact.

What Is Democracy?

Democracy is a complex issue, and there is no universally accepted definition. Most people, however, agree that democracy means majority rule. In *Webster's New World Dictionary* (second college edition, 1980, Simon and Schuster), *democracy* has five similar shades of meaning to cover the principles of democracy:

- government by the people, exercised either directly or through elected representatives
- a country, state, etc. with such a government
- majority rule with the protection of minorities
- the principle of equality of rights, opportunity, and treatment (PEROT) or the practice of this principle
- the common people, especially as the wielders of political power

Entry 1: Government by the People Exercised Either Directly or through Elected Representatives

In Athenian city-states (around 550 BC), democracy was exercised directly where nonslave male citizens who had completed military training voiced their opinions and voted directly at town meetings. In modern times, even a small town is many times larger than the Greek city-states, and democracy is exercised through elected representatives.

Entry 2: A Country, State, Etc. with Such a Government That Is Produced through Democratic Election

Entry 3: Majority Rule with the Protection of Minorities

A democratic government is composed of representatives elected by a majority of the eligible voters; otherwise, it is not a majority rule. However, the protection of minorities is essential since the truth could be with the minorities. For instance, in history, heliocentric belief was once a minority theory and only became a majority belief centuries later.

Entry 4: The Principle of Equality of Rights, Opportunity, and Treatment (PEROT) or the Practice of this Principle

The PEROT is the premise of both democracy and freedom. Without the equality of rights, opportunity and treatment, democracy and freedom are simply unimaginable.

Of course, men are created different with numerous physical and psychological features. Here, the PEROT means no matter how diverse their natural features are, human beings are all equal before the law, in human rights, in opportunity, and in treatment. They are all equal in human dignity and respect. They are all equal in humanity and the pursuit of happiness.

Entry 5: The Common People Are the Wielders of Political Power

This is the core of democracy: the common people are the wielders of political power. The simple facts that 1.3 billion people are struggling in the sea of poverty and a child dies every few seconds prove democracy is far from being exercised as defined above, not to mention ongoing political unrests almost everywhere.

What is the problem? Let us investigate how a contemporary "democratic" government is produced.

The Production of a Contemporary "Democratic" Government

Undemocratic political systems produce governments without free elections. These systems are becoming—or will soon become—historically outdated. Here, we examine only democracies. Contemporary democratic political systems produce governments by electing representatives free of foul play. Election consists of campaigning and voting.

Direct Democracy

The earliest documented direct democracy was Athenian city-states in ancient Greece around 550 BC. In Athenian democracy, only nonslave, nonforeign, military-trained male citizens could vote for legislature and its execution. The voters could speak out and consequently be heard and debated; nowadays, we may compare it to community meetings held for hearing important issues in communities. Even small towns are many times larger than Athenian city-states.

The Athenian direct democracy existed for only 128 years. Like everything else, any invention has its limit. An invasion from Macedonia by Alexander the Great (356–323 BC) was the primary cause.

Inspiringly, while any creation has its limit—birth, growth, and death—its innate reasonable elements would not perish, but they could be born again thousands of years later.

Contemporary Democracy

The fact that modern cities and towns are many times larger than the Athenian city-states makes it impossible to exercise direct democracy. Instead voters elect representatives to do so indirectly for them. This means voters do not propose, discuss, and debate issues directly as in the Athenian city-states.

A problem naturally arises: while voters in general may know what the issues are, they do not specifically know their candidates. In modern times, it is quite common that people who live in the same building may not have spoken to each other once in a lifetime—they are "too busy" to socialize.

Most voters find it easy to watch television to learn something about the candidates. This situation results in whichever candidate appears more on television wins.

Television presentation, the major tool for political campaigns, is expensive. The average cost of a thirty-second nationwide primetime presentation in the United States is over $100,000. Since the goal is to reach every voter nationwide, television presentation should be nationwide and as frequent as possible. As a result, the price can reach astronomical figures. In the 2012 presidential campaign, $2 billion was spent.

Political candidates need a lot of money to finance their campaigns, and they spend a lot of time raising it. There are basically three types of political campaign financing: public financing, private financing, and a combination of both.

Deprivation of the Principle of Equality of Rights

No matter whether the campaign funding is public, private, or a combination of both, few candidates can have it or get it. This divides the population into two classes. Only a few can afford the ultraexpensive modern media; the vast majority can speak but cannot be heard. This is the most severe deprivation of the fundamentals of democracy to the majority. PEROT is the premise of both freedom and democracy.

The essence of democracy is that common people are the wielders of political power. In Athenian democracy, common people expressed, communicated, and debated on the premise that they could speak out, be heard, and be equally treated. Contemporary democracy only allows a few candidates to be heard on television.

Imagine having one huge hall that can accommodate one million people instead of one million people with television sets being scattered in their homes in many cities and towns. In this huge hall, only few citizens speak, debate on numerous television sets, and can be heard. What are the rest of the million people doing in the hall? Some are shouting but cannot be heard, some are setting themselves on fire to send out a protesting message, and others are hopelessly doing nothing since the hall is too big and they cannot afford a television presence to offer or defend their opinions. This is a scary scene for it is like a psychologically abnormal human world.

Problems of Contemporary Democracy

Today, political candidates cannot be heard unless they can afford a media presence. This discourages many potentially good politicians, but it can also drive those candidates to go all out in seeking all possible financing sources to reach their goals. Realizing this genuine need, different governments may provide different campaign-financing support. Besides public financing, rich individuals and big companies may also contribute too. This is private financing.

A problem with campaign financing is that those who receive it may lose political independence. They may no longer feel free to do what they originally wanted to do for the benefit of the public, but they feel obligated to do what the campaign financers think they should do first, which benefits the financers instead of the public. This explains why governments lack the transparency that voters want. The entanglement of politics and business not only darkens the transparency of governments but also opens the door to corruption. This situation may change the mental state of elected officials. The top priority is to remain safely and prosperously in office and get reelected again and again before they see what they can do for the public.

Campaign-financing laws have been enacted to limit excessive contributive donations to address this problem. Some offenders have been punished. Still, because of the intense contests and the cost of the media, illegal financing may keep going in various covert forms. However, the most serious aspect of campaign financing is that it violates PEROT by granting very few candidates the right to be heard.

Democracy and freedom of expression are inalienable human rights—not commodities for sale. The investigative writer Greg Palast put it in *The Best Democracy Money Can Buy* (Pluto Press, London, 2002; Plume Printing, 2003).

Results explain all. Is contemporary democracy working well? Worldwide, the answer is no. Why? If it worked well, the world would not be in such a state with 1.3 billion people struggling in the sea of poverty and a child dying every few seconds, not to mention unrest, conflicts, and wars. This means the UNUDHR has not been implemented effectively by the constitutions of the United Nations member states. This means the key of the UNUDHR "brotherhood equality" is not working.

Indifferent Voters

When voters have voted and watched this practice of contemporary democracy year after year, finally they get enlightened. What does this democracy have to do with them? The answer is that it has very little or nothing to do with them. Most voters have numerous problems to resolve—safety, job security, housing, food, children, medical insurance, education, retirement, and the pursuit of personal dreams, such as owning a house, which may be in foreclosure. When time passes, voters may lose their enthusiasm and expectations of something good; instead, they stop voting or become indifferent to voting. There is nothing exciting to vote for in an election because it is a repeat of an old disappointment. Complete political reforms are inevitable.

NOTES

CHAPTER 4

REFORM CHOICES

There must be grave structural flaws in the political-economic-legal system in a world where there are endless bloody conflicts, refugee exoduses, and massive poverty. When a child dies every few seconds, reform is imperative.

Drastic political reform usually appeals to violence, which is a breaking point of human patience. Violence, however, may create new problems, such as disruption of the normal social order, which most people do not want. It can create complications or irreconcilable hatred, and it can open a door to new autocracy. Furthermore, violence is not the norm of daily life that should be in blissful peace. This is the most horrible bloody lesson humankind has ever learned from World War II, and it is determined never to repeat it with the adoption of the UNUDHR.

Another way to approach the political reform is to present the cause of structural flaws reasonably with the belief that most people are reasonable and will learn to act according to reason. Current world affairs make it easy to believe political reform in the twenty-first century will lead to democracies that are self-cleansing, self-rejuvenating, and self-perfecting. Once water stops running, it becomes bad.

In chapter 3, political-economic-legal defects are presented as long-standing facts that little can be done about. Further investigation reveals the UNUDHR is missing some fundamental human rights—and so are the constitutions of the member states of the United Nations.

Missing Fundamental Human Rights

1) Freedom of Information

More than ninety countries have enacted laws granting citizens general rights to access information held by governments. There are many restrictions on these laws that allow arbitrary explanations and actions, and there are also many modifications since the Freedom of Information (FOI) is not clearly defined. Such loopholes open doors to serious violation of the FOI. Here are some examples:

If a president were assassinated, people were told the truth would be made public seventy years later. It means people had to wait seventy years to know the truth. Seventy years later, most people would no longer exist. This means most people who demanded an answer to the assassination of the president they had elected had no right to know the truth; only those who could live another seventy years would know it as a "historical story."

A majority of qualified voters elect the president through democratic election. People have the right to know since they are the wielders of political power in a democratic system. It was unclear who has the authority to seal the secret—and why and how they have it. If a crime as big as the assassination of a president can be kept a "secret," what about smaller crimes that can be kept "secret" for protection? Jesse Ventura, former governor of Minnesota, published two *New York Times* bestselling books on issues kept secret (*American Conspiracy* and *63 Documents the Government Doesn't Want You To Read*, Jesse Ventura with Dick Russell, Skyhorse Publishing, 2011).

In contemporary times, there are so many things the public cannot possibly know or understand. For instance, tax codes range from several thousand pages to more than ten thousand pages, depending on the country. Albert Einstein, *TIME* magazine's Person of the Century, admitted, "The hardest thing in the world was to understand was the income tax" (irs.gov). If a great genius such as Einstein—who changed the concept of time and space—could not understand the income tax, who can?

This incomprehensible complexity naturally leads to nontransparency and corruption. A former housekeeper testified that she heard Leona Helmsley, an American businesswoman and real estate entrepreneur nicknamed "Queen of Mean," saying only little people paid taxes. In a sense, this brings the twenty-first century back to the Middle Ages when commoners, peasants, and serfs paid taxes to protect their lords. Who are the lords protected in the twenty-first century? And why?

It is clear that the FOI is about the people's right to know the violation of democracy, who is responsible, and how people wield political power to defend democracy.

2) Right to Be Heard in Political Campaigns

Article 18 and article 19 of the UNUDHR are about the rights of freedom of thought and freedom of opinion and expression.

In the UNUDHR and the constitutions of the United Nations member states, people's equal and inalienable rights to freedom of expression are granted. Freedom of expression, like all freedoms, also has certain restrictions; for instance, one should not cry "fire" when there is no fire. But, there is *no fee* whatsoever required for exercising such rights.

In reality, as studied in chapter 3, political candidates must pay hundreds of thousands of dollars for thirty-second nationwide presentations. Otherwise, the public cannot hear them on television or other high-tech media—no matter how wonderful their ideas are. When available, free government media services and public funding are so limited in scope and time that they are not even adequate for political parties, not to mention common people who are supposed to be the wielders of political power in democracies.

This makes it impossible for common people to enjoy the freedom of expression and contribute to political campaigns, disregarding how important their ideas could be. But the freedom of expression for a political campaign is the most important freedom of expression. Why?

Francis Bacon said, "History makes man wise." History teaches humankind that totalitarian regimes killed freedom of expression by massacring ideological dissidents by the million because they didn't think the same way as one lone dictator did. This dictator usually was worshipped as holy. In ancient superstitions, he sacrificed lives and put them on altars to please his gods, thus creating the darkest periods in the history of civilization. What we need is just the opposite. We need to change ideology and improve human life—not sacrifice human lives to defend ideology, no matter how great it appears, because ideology is only a product of the human mind. This is why the freedom of expression is critical in political campaigns.

London's Hyde Park and American Idol

In London's Hyde Park, people can make free speeches about whatever they want. Those who make speeches in this park must desperately need to pour out what is on their minds. Sometimes there are not even any listeners around, but the speakers still go on with their speeches.

In the United States, *American Idol* is a program where singers compete with one another for the best performance on television. This is followed by nationwide voting via phones. Those who get the majority of votes continue the next day.

3) Free Government Political Media (FGPM)

The spontaneous practice of freedom of speech in London's Hyde Park, more than 2,500 years after the Athenian city-states direct democracy in Greece, reminds us that direct democracy is not dead. Like scientists reviving and restoring species from a single gene of the lost species, is it possible to restore direct democracy? Yes, we can. *American Idol* shows how we can overcome the difficulty of scattered populations that are too large to practice direct democracy with the help of modern technology. We need to open Free Government Political Media (FGPM).

The FGPM program means governments should give free media access on all government levels to all qualified citizens who want to criticize, suggest, and campaign for office on a first-come, first-served basis—free of charge. The media includes television, radio, Internet,

Facebook, Twitter, YouTube, and all state-of-the art high-technology tools. The FGPM should be open all the time because people may work at different hours. The more people participate, the more democratic it will be. After each presentation, there will be a vote to determine who will continue the next day. The winner will advance to a higher level of FGPM.

This is to defend the PEROT; the practice of this principle is the premise of freedom and democracy. Freedom of expression in political campaigns must be complemented with the right to be heard. In our high-tech world, it can be done effortlessly if the FGPM is fully understood and accepted like Hyde Park and *American Idol* are.

The United Nations and all its member states should adopt new articles and enact new laws regarding FGPM, the UNUDHR, and the constitutions of all member states of the United Nations.

4) Equal Inalienable Human Rights Are Not for Sale

The FGPM protects the principle of equality of rights because inalienable human rights are not commodities that can be bought economically or politically. While giving a chance to all qualified citizens, the FGPM frees would-be politicians from the yoke of big-money donations and political favoritism. They can use wisdom, compassion, and courage in a fair way. If fairly carried out, highly qualified candidates will emerge since there are about seven billion people in the world.

Democratic Genetic Engineering

Never promote democracy by war. Always promote democracy and freedom by example. Only the United Nations has the right to interfere militarily, according to the resolution supported by majority of member states. To kill in God's name, one needs a certified approval signature from God.

A society is made of numerous units that we can metaphorically call cells. These cells form the building blocks of society. The democratization of all the cells forms the democratization of the whole society.

In this sense, democratic genetic engineering (DGE) means all cells observe the same democratic principles, including the following issues:

1) Three Independent Power Branches

All authorities should be composed of three independent branches: legislative, judicial, and executive. Leaders of these three branches should be produced by periodical democratic election processes. None of them should be produced by appointments.

2) Democratic Decision Making

Every important decision, such as war or peace, should be made through democratic processes—that is, two votes out of the three branches are required to make a decision. All undemocratic decisions are unlawful.

3) Free Speech Forum

Following the principles of FGPM, governments at all levels should have their own FGPM while all nongovernmental units should open a free speech forum (FSF) for people to know, speak out, and be heard. This is critical since the whole society is composed of cells. The health of these cells is the foundation of all structures built upon these basic units.

Why Do We Need DGE?

1) To Attain Political Independence and Open Political Consciousness

Politics may be influenced by many factors, including money, traditions, and religious beliefs. The FGPM of DGE provides a great chance for attaining political independence and making politicians independent.

Many people think it is not worth it to spend time and effort on politics since they can do nothing about it. However, there must be some people who want to speak their minds once they get the chance to present it on the FGPM. These lively examples will open a new optimistic perspective to all. A new time has come.

2) Motivate People to Engage in Politics

The DGE will revolutionize political life. Common people who might think it is the politicians' job to do politics might be motivated to realize that it is their very responsibility to get involved in politics. Politics is too important to leave to the politicians.

Once they have tried, people will be surprised by their achievements. People will be working for themselves and will be motivated to search for all possible solutions to real issues in their lives. The politicians may be working for special interest groups before the people. No matter how difficult the issues are, there will be solutions after many debates and exchanges of creative, constructive, cooperative opinions.

3) Eliminate Institutionalized Bureaucracy

This is an inherited, appointed power structure without renewal from periodic democratic elections. Fossils are better off in museums than running the real lives of people. Now the DGE provide a chance to renew it.

(*Dynamic Chikung*, ibid)

4) Reveal Facts about Political Truths

When people exercise their rights and freedoms to know, speak, and be heard without fear, they tell the facts about political truths they know that are being covered up for unknown reasons. Political knowledge based on facts is critical for making policy.

Also, this is critical for cleaning government agencies and corporations at all levels. No corruption or scandal can be hidden from all people all the time. Only people who are involved know the details and will disclose unlawful facts once they believe their rights and personal security are surely protected.

5) Reveal Facts about Economic Truth

This is to uncover and verify facts about the economy that are covered up for unknown reasons. Economic knowledge based on facts may influence all aspects of everyone's life and the nation's life as well.

It is critical to identify real social needs. In a free-market consumer society, manufacturers often generate needs by advertising. When the economy is not doing well, consumers would better off cutting back on man-generated needs to return to genuine needs, such as housing, food, clothing, transportation, medical insurance, and education. This will give manufacturers helpful information for operating their businesses according to social needs and more.

When time passes, a political culture will be formed that will likely change the political atmosphere and permeate everywhere, cultivating political consciousness. It is everyone's responsibility to take politics into their own hands. "The common people, especially, are the wielders of political power."

6) Defend the Principle of Equality of Rights, Opportunity, and Treatment (PEROT)

FGPM is supposed to run all the time so that working people can use it. Following the PEROT, it should be on a first-come, first-served basis. When a presentation has been made, voting will be held via phones, computer programs, social media, and state-of-the-art devices. The votes will determine whether the presentation will continue or discontinue. The final winner on one level of FGPM will advance to a higher level of FGPM. In this way, political campaigns are going on all the time.

In the beginning, this free program will attract numerous people in a chaotic way. They may want to pour out bitter memories as a result of undemocratic treatment. Since this apparent popularity will create great positive pressure on the government and all involved institutions to resolve the issues, gradually the number of the issues will decrease with the increase of successful solutions, order and efficiency will gradually firmly prevail, and a democratic free political culture will be established based on the execution of the PEROT in entry 4 of the definition of democracy, and common people will become the wielders of political powers as in entry 5.

7) Unite a Separated Society

In the UNUDHR, the key word is "brotherhood." This key word is the crystallization of the blood of sixty million victims during World II. But the fact is most people are lonely and isolated; many don't even have a family.

There are many people struggling for survival in our contemporary world. They are too busy with their own problems. It is common for people residing in the same building to not know one another. They feel so lonely and out of touch with the world after a day's work—if they even have jobs. Others don't even have the chance to organize a family. The homeless are the most miserable.

Loneliness and isolation can happen to well-off people. At least they do not feel they are living in a world of brotherhood. This is not what human beings should be. We should be able to be social beings enjoying brotherhood.

The DGE program creates situations that engage people in social activities through participation in discussions and debates that lead to constructive cooperation for solving common concerns on a daily basis. In this interaction, people gradually find they share the same destinies and fates. The best way to address our common problems is to treat each other in brotherhood and unite together.

Petition to Representatives

Democracy is one of the most important human rights. It must not be a product of a gun or money or a political slogan. The dictatorship of a gun or the purchase of democracy by money or political propaganda must be stopped. The DGE needs to be enacted by legislature. Every citizen is encouraged to submit a petition to his or her elected representatives.

NOTES

CHAPTER 5

LESSONS FROM NATURE

The democratic genetic engineering program has its profound cognitive sources in the real world. The most realistic world is nature. Man is part of nature. We study, test, and learn from nature to discover its secrets. We apply the laws we have learned from nature to conquer nature. Nature is our teacher.

Can Man Recognize the Truth?

Many culprits are blamed for the world financial crisis: obscene greed, universal corruption, scandalous government deregulations, and fantasies illusively taken as reality, etc. This is mostly related to government financial officers, financial institute executives, entrepreneurs, CEOs, and stock market gurus who are involved directly in the financial field for duty or profits.

We have Nobel-winning economists, professors, and academic research experts who are not directly involved in making money, but they search for the truth to guide financial activities in the right direction. None of them predicted a crisis of this scale and duration, but some warned of an ominous economic situation. More preparation could have avoided many human tragedies.

- Can we recognize the truth?
- If we can, why did we fail this time?

31

- How can we improve cognitive ability to prevent similar crises in the future?

The Limit of Human Cognitive Ability

Humankind is intelligent. People observe, investigate, experiment, test, and take action. The consequence of people's actions depends upon the accuracy of their knowledge of the laws of the objective world—and the way they carry out what has been learned and blueprinted. In this process, no one can be completely correct no matter how intelligent he or she is. In fact, people have to make corrections whenever or wherever needed in the process of the realization of the plan. This process can be categorized as an integration of the subjective world with the objective world. People learn laws from the objective world that guide them to realize subjective goals. In this sense, we can say subjective goals and the objective world are becoming one.

A problem stealthily arises. Humankind has a limited existence in space-time, and the objective world and its laws are infinite. This is an eternal contradiction that makes life seem tragic. Finite life is pursuing infinite knowledge to vainly quench the innate, everlasting thirst for Truth, Goodness, and Beauty.

It was not random that the Greek philosopher Socrates (469–399 BC) said, "I know nothing except the fact of my ignorance." His prize student was Plato (429–347 BC). Plato's prize student was Aristotle (384–322 BC). Aristotle laid the foundation of Western philosophy and science.

Greece has produced great philosophers who were honored by the entire world. But if we watch the current Greece antiausterity mass protests that started more than a year ago, we can understand that what Socrates said is true: People even do not know their ignorance. Otherwise, such mass protests could be predicted, prevented, or resolved.

In the East, the Chinese philosopher Lao Tse (500 – 400 BC) expressed similar infinity of knowledge. He wrote, "To know you don't know is best. Not to know you [don't] know is a flaw." (*Tao Te Ching*, Robert G. Henricks, 1993 Modern Library Edition, 175.)

Lao Tse opened the *Tao Te Ching* (*Dao De Jing*), one of the most published books in the world, by saying, "The Tao (Truth) can be told, not the constant Tao (Truth)."

The original Chinese text has only six Chinese words, but they might be the six most important Chinese words ever written. These words inspire people to search for new truths on a continuous basis—no matter what has already been achieved. This is extremely critical to understand the nature of Truth.

There are numerous translations of the *Tao Te Ching*, which implies how difficult a good translation can be. A professor at San Francisco State University, Jacob Needleman, wrote, "The word Tao, and even the whole of the Tao Te Ching, are not readily translatable into any language, including Chinese!" (*Introduction to the Tao Te Ching*, Gia-Fu Feng and Jane English, Vintage Books Edition, August 1989).

According to Lao Tse, the Tao (Truth) can be told. But the Tao (Truth) is not a static Tao (Truth). It is a dynamic one. This means it has to be updated with new discoveries. Tao (Truth) is a process at each stage of which the human mind can discover only a transitional Tao (Truth) but not the final Tao (Truth). Human life is limited in space-time, but the Tao (Truth) is infinite. This completely agrees with the history of natural science where nothing is final. While the truth is a process, it is wrong to regard the truth—transitional by nature—as something static and free from new discoveries.

The history of natural science confirms Lao Tse's point of view on the truth. The British physicist Isaac Newton (1642–1727), one of the fathers of modern physics, was perhaps the greatest scientist ever lived. In his time, there was even a saying that God created the world, and Newton explained the world. Newton could predict the motion of the planets by applying his famous three laws of motion. He was praised by some of his contemporaries as the spokesman of God.

When he was asked to talk about himself during an interview, he said, "I do not know what I may seem to the world, but as to myself, I seem to have been only like a boy playing on the seashore and diverting myself in now and then finding a smoother pebble or a prettier shell than ordinary, whilst the great ocean of truth lay all undiscovered before me (Joseph Spence Anecdotes (ed. J. Osborn, 1966) no. 1259, *Oxford Dictionary of Quotations, Sixth Edition*).

Newton confirmed he had found "in now and then a smoother pebble or a prettier shell than ordinary," which means he had found some small truths while "the great ocean of truth all lay undiscovered before him." This is close to what Lao Tse said.

Now we know that Newton was right. His theory is not accurate when applying to an object at a speed close to that of light (299792.5 km/per second or 186282.4 miles per second). It should be replaced by the theory of relativity of Albert Einstein (1879–1955). When the object is at the atomic or subatomic level, Newton's theory should be replaced by quantum mechanics, which, based on experimental data, believes that our knowledge about an individual event at the subatomic level is only a probability. The average of numerous individual micro-subatomic events, however, constitutes a macroscopic event.

The replacement of an older theory by a newer discovery makes up the history of natural sciences. If a scientifically well-established object such as Pluto—which was considered the solar system's ninth planet from its discovery in 1930 until 2006—could be excluded as a planet according to new scientific discoveries, we can expect many more in nonscientific issues. There must be an enormous amount of false beliefs, prejudices, and obsolete knowledge in the human mind that we hold as the truth.

Tao Follows Nature

Lao Tse says, "The Earth follows the Heaven, the Heaven follows the Tao (Truth), and the Tao (Truth) follows Nature." The first thing we have to do is to identify reality, which is the starting point of all further investigations.

A prominent scientist, Ilya Prigogine (1917–2003) who won the Nobel Prize in 1977 for his work on thermodynamics of nonequilibrium systems, wrote about the future way of thinking in *Order out of Chaos* with Isabelle Stengers (Bantam Books, 1984).

> *Perhaps we will eventually be able to combine the Western tradition, with its emphasis on experimentation and quantitative formulations, with a tradition such as the Chinese one, with its view of a spontaneous, self-organizing world.*

Such an awesome task may take decades even to begin, but we can find the revelations and inspirations provided by natural sciences.

Experimentation is the foundation of what we call science that originated in the West. A pure idea is only subjective and has no objective truth if not confirmed by experimentation—no matter how holy, scholarly, or traditional it is.

Experimentation is the bridge between subjectivity and objectivity, which leads to the discovery of the truth. There is no substitute for experimentation.

Scientific experimentation is conducted on objects, and the results acquired should be universally valid. When repeating an experiment under the same conditions, the results should be the same. When experimenting on freedom and democracy, the objects are people. The universality of freedom and democracy should be verified by positive responses from a majority of the voting population as required by the majority rule of democracy. There should be a communication mechanism that automatically records the support or rejection quantitatively as pointed out by Prigogine. The GFPM is one of such programs.

1) Impartial Natural Science

Natural science is based on experimentation that is impartial to all, no matter if a person is a king or a pauper. Unfortunately, it is not always true since the interpretation of the natural science might mean gain or loss to certain vested special interests.

The Polish astronomer Nicolaus Copernicus (1473–1543) was the first to formulate a heliocentric cosmology that replaced the Sun with the Earth as the center of the universe. He hesitated to publish his epoch-making book *De Revolutionibus Orbium Coelestium* (On the Revolutions of the Celestial Spheres) until 1543, just before his death. His work stimulated further scientific investigations, becoming a landmark in the history of modern science that is often referred to as the Copernican Revolution.

The Italian physicist Galileo Galilei (1564–1642) is universally acknowledged as one of the fathers of modern physics. While championing Copernican heliocentric cosmology, he met bitter opposition from Catholic clerics. After he published his most famous work, *Dialogue Concerning the Two Chief World Systems*, in 1632, he was tried by the Inquisition, found "vehemently suspect of heresy," forced to recant, and spent the rest of his life under house arrest. This is a classic example of self-deified, man-made dogma oppressing a science giant and the truth he championed. History soon proved Galileo was correct and was a victim of ignorance.

Freedom of expression is essential to democracy. If a science giant could not freely express his findings about nature in the 1700s and was persecuted by special interest groups' prejudice rooted in ignorance (but coated with holy glamour), can common people express themselves freely about social issues in the twenty-first century in a democracy? Theoretically they can, but practically they cannot. They have to pay the media tremendous amounts of money to be heard—or they have to be politicians representing special interest groups. That is why the FGPM is needed.

This impartiality is the foundation of PEROT is an indispensable feature of democracy. It leads to a one standard rule. Such claims as "I can, but you cannot" or "Mine is mine, yours is also mine" only make things worse. The clarity of thought is extremely critical since we think and weigh before we act. If our thoughts are wrong, prejudiced, partial, our actions will be too. For instance, if the classic statement is not "All men are created equal," but "All men are created equal, including slaves," about one hundred thousand American lives could have been saved.

2) Reliability of Natural Science

When we look closely at human knowledge as a whole, our knowledge of nature is something we can and must accept at least for now. Although Newton's theory is not as accurate as Einstein's theory of relativity when the motion is comparable to the speed of light, it is completely necessary and sufficient in our daily life. If a man does not believe it and wants to cross the traffic flow on a red light or jump from a plane without a parachute, he will certainly be killed by the impact. The laws established by natural sciences are really serious—they may mean the difference between life and death. In the twenty-first century, educated, mentally healthy people don't reject natural science.

When exercising democracy through political elections, most voters feel disappointed after the election. As mentioned before, voters may get a repeat of an old disappointment. Obviously, reliability of natural science is our teacher too. Natural laws never lie.

3) Experimentation Opens New Possibilities

Experimentation is the criterion of truth, but it also opens new ways to creatively address the problems facing humanity.

A) Quantitative Formulation

The greatest experiments conducted in the twentieth century were relativity and quantum mechanics. Albert Einstein, based on previous physical experiments, conducted a thought experiment to analyze the concept of simultaneity. Newtonian concept of space-time and simultaneity was based upon unconfirmed assumptions that space-time was the same everywhere in the universe. Einstein conducted his experiment by analyzing actual transmittals of light signals for the measurements of space-time. From this analysis, which was based on experiments, Einstein established unimaginable results that a moving rod contracts, a moving clock slows down, and a moving mass becomes larger. He further formulated theory of general relativity was confirmed by testing and revolutionarily changed the concept of space-time. *TIME* magazine named him Person of the Century.

Although the relativistic effects, such as contraction of a moving rod, cannot be sensed and visualized by our sense organs, they can be reasoned and quantitatively formulated—and the results can be tested. This opens a new perspective for humanity by making them scientifically testable to provide better information.

B) Synthesis of Opposites Opens New Possibilities

Another unimaginable scientific discovery was the wave-particle duality in quantum mechanics. According to all confirmed experiments, a particle, such as an atom, must be thought of as a particle or as a wave, depending on the way it is examined. While a particle occupies a point in space at a certain moment, a wave occupies the entire space. As a visual example, imagine throwing a stone into a pond. The stone, a particle, enters the water at a certain point, generating a wave in the form of concentric circles that spread out to the entire lake surface. In this case, the stone and the wave are two different objects with different properties, which is thinkable.

Unexplainably, we can hardly imagine a single physical object that has both particle and wave properties at the same time, corresponding to the impossibility of conducting an experiment on both particle and wave properties simultaneously in a physics laboratory. Thus, the particle-like and wavelike properties are mutually exclusive. This duality, nevertheless, seems to be comparable to the Chinese dualistic philosophy of *yin and yang*. Yang is the active, masculine cosmic force, while yin is the passive, opposite, female cosmic force. The difference is that according to the Chinese philosophy, contrary to the wave-particle mutually exclusive dualism, yin and yang are always mutually complementary and transformable into each other.

This understanding of the mutual complementary, transformable nature of yin and yang is so enlightening that Niels Bohr (1885–1962), one of the founders of modern atomic physics and a Nobel Prize laureate

(1922), chose the tai chi symbol featuring a rotating image of yin and yang—the Taoist symbol of the cosmos and once a top secret in the Sung Dynasty (960–1280) when it was first created—as his motif for his coat-of-arms together with the inscription *Contraria sunt complementa* (Opposites are complementary) when he was knighted in 1947 (*The Tao of Physics*, Fritjof Capra, 1984, 145).

When DGE is healthily exercised and becomes the way of modern political life—everyone realizes and exercises his or her rights while letting others do the same on a fair-play basis—there must be more battles between opposites. This seems abnormal, but it is not.

The story about particle-wave dualism in physics may be very unfamiliar to those who have not studied modern physics. In daily life, however, we all know a coin has two sides and flipping a coin leads to an uncertain outcome about which side will show up. The head and the tail of a coin are opposites, but whether the head or the tail will show up is mutually exclusive. This uncertainty makes it possible to create a gambling game based on the wish for good luck. Without two sides, it is impossible. In the sense that the two sides of a coin make up the coin and create a gambling game, they are complementary.

The wave-particle dualism is self-exclusive. This means we cannot have wave and particle at the same time—but either wave or particle alternatively. This self-exclusive dualism does not trigger a war among physicists to resolve the conflict, but it inspired them to create a synthesis of this self-antagonistic physical phenomenon. An Austrian physicist Irwin Schrödinger (1885–1962) synthesized the wave-particle dualism in quantum mechanics in 1926. He proposed a probability wave function governed by the Schrödinger equation, which was named after him. He shared the Nobel Prize in Physics in 1933 with the British physicist Paul A. M. Dirac (1902–1984) who first formulated relativistic quantum mechanics, which predicted an antiparticle to each particle, such as a positron to electron, that has the same mass but opposite charge. Their theories explained and predicted many physics phenomena at atomic and subatomic levels. The synthesis of opposites opens new paths to creatively discover new things.

C) Probability Interpretation

Another critical result from quantum mechanics is that knowledge about individual events at the atomic or subatomic level is no longer a certainty—it is a probability. The average of numerous individual events provides macroscopic knowledge. If we measure a rod with a very precise ruler, we get a different reading every time. In physics, an average is taken over all the different readings and is assumed to be the length of the rod.

Democracy requires majority rule. The more people participate, the more complete the democracy is. The problem is how to obtain an average for all individual participating activities.

The FGPM encourages people to criticize, propose, and debate in order to obtain more truthful and better solutions to existing political, economic, and legal problems.

This is particularly important for the FGPM to generate nonstop debates; the longer the time, the more people can participate.

This is the main difference between a democracy and a nondemocracy. A nondemocracy makes a decision based on an individual's judgment or interest, which can be a random probability that reflects a false situation or a distortion of the truth. On the contrary, real democracy makes a decision through a debating process to reveal the truth.

D) Observation Changes Reality

Furthermore, the wave-particle dualism in quantum mechanics opens a completely new aspect of reality on the relation between the observer and the object under observation. The result of observation is no longer independent from the observer—whether an atom is a particle or a wave depends on the way it is observed. This means the subject becomes a part of the objective world during the process of observation.

This finding is critical to the understanding of what we call democracy—the core of which is that the people are the wielders of political power. Democracy is exercised through an election process.

Voters usually picture themselves electing candidates to represent them to wield political power—but not as wielders of political power themselves.

Since the observer changes the reality he or she observes according to quantum mechanics, we have to be wielders of political power ourselves in order to exercise democracy.

This is not difficult to understand. For instance, if you own a house, you will only feel the difference too soon if you assume the authority yourself instead of dedicating it to someone else who can do whatever he or she likes after the dedication. The same happens in an election. Very few constituents are satisfied with the representatives elected after a successful campaign.

The FGPM provides a chance for every qualified voter to be a political power wielder. Any qualified voter is encouraged to announce his or her candidacy on the FGPM and to promote the best policy he or she can produce to make the country and the world a better place. There will only be one final winner after all the campaigns, but no matter who wins or loses, all of them have become real wielders of political power at certain stage of the process that is the core of democracy, and they have changed the process from a passive one to an active democratic one.

There are many organizations still fighting for civil rights, human rights, and democracy. This means freedom and democracy printed in constitutions of civilized countries do not work well; otherwise, such organizations are not needed. If freedom and democracy only exist in the printed matter of constitutions and are compromised in real life, we are in a real crisis.

Those who fight for democracy can expect democracy that is more than a statement carved on the walls of great halls as part of constitutions. It is what we exercise, measure, and improve in real-life situations since we prefer to be wielders of political power and take the responsibility to make the world a better place. There is an FGPM available. Gradually, democracy will become the way of life and the culture as well.

Interestingly, the ancient Chinese yin yang philosophy is based on the observation that everything has a male (yang) side and a female (yin) side that are necessary to produce something new. An example is a baby. This is creation, which prolongs species.

Open Mind

In Greece, the theory of opposites was called *dialectic* as a method of argument, which has been central to both Eastern and Western philosophy since ancient times. The word *dialectic* originated in ancient Greece, and Plato's *Socratic Dialogue* made it popular. Dialectic is rooted in the ordinary practice of a dialogue between two or more people who hold different ideas but wish to persuade each other. The presupposition of a dialectical argument is that the participants, even if they do not agree, share at least some meanings and principles of inference. Different forms of dialectical reason have emerged in the East and in the West, as well as during different eras of history. Among the major forms of dialectic reason are Socratic, Hindu, Buddhist, Medieval, Hegelian, Marxist, and Talmudic.

It is very important to update a philosophy with the development of natural science because when we define an object, we depend on the ability of recognition, which changes and develops with time. For instance, Pluto was formerly defined as a planet in the solar system, but with the development of science, we found that Pluto is actually a mass of gas. It is not a planet.

Think of Opposites

We usually misunderstand opposites as contradictory and mutually exclusive, without realizing the validity of such a statement is dependent upon the implicit condition assumed in making such a statement.

When we say house A is on the east of house B, it doesn't make sense to say A is on the west of B at the same time. These two statements are mutually exclusive.

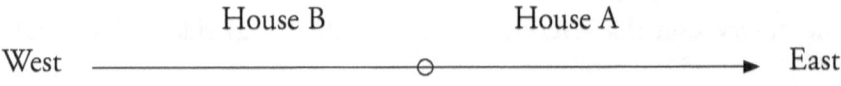

However, when we say San Francisco (SF) is on the west of New York City (NYC), we can also say SF is on the east of NYC. The proof is that when we fly west from NYC, we can reach SF. But if you fly east from NYC, you can also reach SF via the Atlantic Ocean. This is because we look at these two statements from a global point of view, taking into consideration that the Earth is round—and the line connecting SF and NYC is a curve instead of a straight line as assumed in the first case of house A and B. When we say house A is on the east of house B, it doesn't make sense to say A is on the west of B at the same time. These two statements are mutually exclusive. In the second case, when we say SF is on the west of NYC, we can also say SF is on the east of NYC as well. These two statements are complementary. If a hurricane is attacking the west of NYC, flights can go east to reach SF.

Here is an inspiring fact: mutually exclusive opposites can be consistent if considered from a wider perspective. Generally speaking, thinking of opposites is to open the mind to discover new things or create new solutions to old problems. This is very important to understand we really have more things in common than differences—and we are in brotherhood as stated in the UNUDHR. This understanding will greatly expand the capacity of tolerance, receptivity, and constructive cooperation to create a more harmonious world.

San Francisco

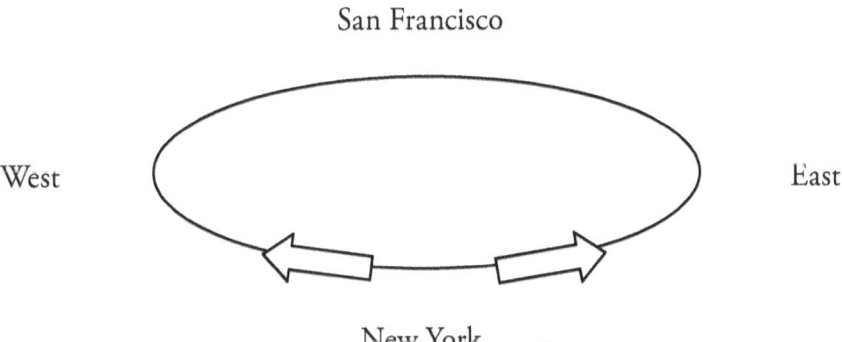

West   East

New York

A coin has two sides. When flipping a coin, we can only get the head or the tail, but not both at the same time: they are contradictory and mutually exclusive. But the coin is made of two sides, and there is no coin that has only one side. In making up the coin, the head and tail sides are opposite but complementary.

When we say this is a book, we imply it is not a pen, or a pencil, etc. This series is inexhaustibly infinite. "It is a book" is only an assumption since we cannot list all nonbook items. Again, the truth of a book is only a probability. This suggests that quantum mechanics is correct about human knowledge that is only probable.

It is not random that there is a saying, "The greatest enemy is self." It happens often that our judgment about our opponent is right while our judgment about self is wrong. It also is not random that the Bible says, "Love your enemy."

War or Peace

As described before, the physical world is built upon particle-wave mutually exclusive dualism, like two sides of a coin. These opposites are complementary. Misunderstanding of this basic dualistic property, however, influences and manifests itself in every aspect of life. The most convincing evidence is war.

In wars, people believe they have more irresolvable conflicts than common interests, which can be resolved only by violence. Human civilization has suffered from numerous wars, and the deadliest was World War II with about sixty million killed. Albert Einstein said he didn't know what weapons would be used in World War III, but he did know people would fight with stones in World War IV.

In 1948, the United Nations passed the UNUDHR in the hopes of putting an end to all wars for good by declaring human rights, particularly the right for life. However, a cold war between the capitalist world and the communist world started even before the declaration was adopted. World peace had been in great danger with a real possibility of annihilation of humankind in a nuclear war—if human conscience and common sense had been completely dead.

Numerous authors have written about war. Among these authors, Sun Tzu (544–496 BC) wrote *The Art of War* based on about 250 years of experience of practical wars in the so-called seven Warring States in China (475–221 BC). Some scholars comment that *The Art of War* is the best book ever written since any violation of its principles leads to failure. According to Sun Tzu, war is the last resort after all political and diplomatic measures have failed and the state is under attack.

The Warring States waged wars against one another for more than two centuries. Numerous people perished or suffered from pains beyond description. When a male child was born, he had already been enrolled as a soldier or a laborer. His future destiny was to fight the war for his emperor until his death.

This entire catastrophe was driven by a single concept—to restore the Mandate of Heaven, which meant to unite China into one empire. After years of bloody wars, the first Chinese Emperor Qin Shi Huang (259–210 BC) conquered the other Warring States and united China. He burned books and buried 246 scholars alive in the fear that knowledge and thought could start a revolution. Thus he began the feudalistic autocracy rule that lasted thousands of years.

If the Warring States had changed their concept by acknowledging one another as independent states, China probably would have developed into something like Europe. There would be much more freedom and development and a much less centralized bureaucracy. The nations and their people would be much better off. Even Mao admitted it shortly before his death in 1976. The Mandate of Heaven was not feudalistic unification as believed; it was about freedom and democracy.

Here is an interesting historical lesson for all. Strangely enough, the time of the Warring States was the most prosperous period for Chinese thought and ideology. At that time, there were two slogans: "Let one hundred flowers bloom" and "Let one hundred schools contend." Even today, every educated Chinese feels nostalgic about losing something most precious.

However, the rulers did not like it. In addition to Emperor Qin Shi Huang burning books and burying the scholars alive, Emperor Han Wu-Ti (157–87 BC) of the Han Dynasty abolished all schools to honor Confucianism alone and made it a state philosophy. Confucianism is great even judged from modern understanding, but once it became a state philosophy, freedom of thought and expression was dead.

From that time on, Chinese intellectuals studied the classics of Confucius to pass the state examination and become government officers with an attitude of looking down upon anything else. About two thousand years later, the First Opium War (1839–1842) proved the state philosophy policy was completely wrong. We need open minds and to think of opposites. This lesson is good for all since China has a long history and is the most populous country in the world.

After the proclamation of the UNUDHR, in addition to the cold war between the capitalist and the communist worlds, many wars were going on, including some wars that are still going. This fact illustrates that the "win-or-lose" solution is not a proper solution to conflicts comprised of opposites like the two sides of a coin. Today, you flip a coin and get a head; tomorrow, you flip it and get a tail. This can go on forever, which precludes peace and stability, which are one of the most critical conditions for life and prosperity.

This applies to the war on terrorism, which is based on an ideology. A material force cannot conquer an ideology that is a spiritual entity. On the contrary, it can help spread it. Terrorists are human beings with different religious beliefs, but they also believe in natural sciences. Will this open the path to constructive debate based on the UNUDHR and indisputable scientific facts to reach understanding for peace?

Make Wings to Fly

When driving a car, we want to minimize air resistance as much as possible. But resistance exists no matter how effectively aerodynamics is applied. The effort of designing an ideal car never ends.

The Wright brothers, Orville (1871–1948) and Wilbur (1867–1912), approached this problem in an entirely different way. They put wings on a machine they invented called a plane and applied the aerodynamics formula established by Bernoulli (1700–1782). In this way, they revolutionized the entire transportation industry by thinking and complementing opposites: air still is resistance to the forward motion of the plane, but it is also a lifting power that enables the plane to fly in straight lines in space, making travel much faster. This has revolutionized the entire transportation industry.

Fly without Wings to Freedom

A plane can fly in air only. Without air, there is no lifting power to the plane. But rocket scientists use the reaction. According to Newton's three laws of motion, every action generates an opposite reaction of the same magnitude. If you throw a heavy object from a little floating boat, the boat will move in the opposite direction of the thrown object. This is due to the reaction to the action of the thrown object. So by jetting burning fuels to the Earth, a rocket can carry a satellite to leave the Earth and orbit around the Earth in airless outer space freely.

The backward fuel ejection of the rocket is complemented by the forward motion of the rocket, just as the freedom of speech is complemented by the "right to be heard" through FGPM.

Gun Control Problem

Gun control is a worldwide problem, though the United States is suffering from gun crimes more than other industrialized countries. There are never-ending debates about assault weapons, people's rights to bear arms according to the United States Constitution, etc. With "thinking opposites" in mind, it is not difficult to realize "assault" and "defend" are mutually transforming, like flipping of two sides of a coin. When automatic assault weapons are banned, a single pistol can become an assault weapon to kill people.

In a civilized society, people enjoy freedom unless they have committed a crime and are proven guilty by trial. People have the right to life, and any killing is illegal without a trial. This lawful understanding naturally leads to abolishing all weapons with the ability to kill—no matter assault or defensive. This means all weapons should be converted to nonkilling, only temporarily debilitating weapons to protect people's rights to life. This principle is also extendable internationally to all nations. The goal of the UNUDHR is eternal peace and brotherhood.

CHAPTER 6

LET HUMAN DREAMS COME TRUE

Human beings dream. Realization of dreams creates civilization. It is one of the most distinctive features that differs human beings from all other forms of life. A baby may dream of its mother's breast, a child may dream of a toy, a teenager may dream of the opposite sex, an unemployed person dreams of a job, a homeless person dreams of a home, anyone may dream of fortune and fame. No matter whether the dream is fanciful or realistic, there is something of great value in the simple fact that human beings dream.

As said before, in the world financial crisis, the Arab Spring, the Occupy Wall Street movement, political unrest and demonstrations, and bloody civil wars, many people perished because of the violence or by taking their own lives by self-immolation to send a message. Others simply could not bear the humiliation of being unemployed. All these issues are addressed in detail in the UNUDHR, but it is not implemented well due to internal structural flaws and should be complemented by DGE.

Resistance to Change

In physics, Newton's first law of motion states a body remains at rest or in motion with a constant velocity unless acted upon by an external force. It is also called the law of inertia, which means resistance to change. To some extent, the same holds true in social behavior.

In society, people promote or resist changes according to evaluation and expectations of gains or losses that changes will probably bring about. Their main consideration is to keep possessions.

Possessed by Possession

DGE will bring drastic change to everyone's lives. As something completely new, it certainly will encounter a lot of resistance. The core of all resistance is the fear of losing possession.

Possession provides livelihood, security, satisfaction, and social recognition, including fantasy. Possession could be a result of lifetime achievements, continuous effort and ingenuity, and good luck. It could also be inherited from ancestors who are loved and remembered. Naturally, we hold to it dearly. It is hard to detach from it as if it were part of life itself. In this sense, we can even say, "We are partially possessed by possession."

Waste of Possession

A possession can either be in use, idle, or in between. When it is in use, especially in good use, it is what the possession is meant to be. When it is not in use, which unfortunately happens very often, it is not what a possession meant to be. It is a waste. This includes talent, which is a precious possession.

When we put a possession to work in the way we like, we feel the possession is worth the effort. Otherwise, we feel the possession is not worth the effort. In this case, possession can be a burden.

Life Is Limited, and Possessions Are Not Portable

Life seems tragic because it is limited, and possession is not portable. A person may leave nothing substantial when leaving this beautiful world or a fortune that can feed millions. In our strange world, a study by the World Institute for Development Economics Research at United Nations University reports that the richest 1 percent of the world's adults alone owned 40 percent of global assets in 2000. The three richest people possessed more financial assets than the lowest forty-eight nations combined. (http://en.wikipedia.org/wiki/Economic_inequality)

Fortunately, there is no such thing as three sheep occupying more pastures than forty-eight sheep nations combined; otherwise, there would be constant sheep wars in nature.

While the ultrarich consume maybe one-billionth of their possessions, people usually consume only a small portion of what they possess.

Systematic Approach of Targeted Philanthropy

Philanthropy is love of mankind, practical sympathy, and actively helping humanity. Philanthropists are humanitarians who work for the welfare of human beings. Usually they are successful entrepreneurs who believe life is limited, possession is not portable, and a possession should be in good use. Experienced and knowing how to succeed, they believe it is meaningful to donate what they can to make a better world by helping people in need and developing their potential to make a better world. Inspiringly, there is a long list of world philanthropists— and the list is becoming longer each day. Although an individual's life span is limited, his or her contribution to philanthropy will last. Some philosophers and poets describe it like how a drop of water will never dry up in a huge ocean. This is human spiritual immortality that will stay.

In the history of civilization, many giants have made unmeasured contributions to the world through creativity or discovery. Talent is a most valuable possession that should be developed completely to be a source of supreme happiness, to bear fruits for the world and flourish for many generations to come, and stay there for many generations to come.

Coordination of Philanthropy

Philanthropists are outstanding entrepreneurs; otherwise they cannot contribute as philanthropists usually do. But the world is big, and they need to organize and coordinate their resources and efforts in an efficient way to realize their sublime intentions.

It will be inspiring for world philanthropists to get together and establish their organization and coordinate with the United Nations to spare duplicate efforts. This will set up an outstanding example of *brotherhood*, the spiritual key to all the thirty articles in the UNUDHR. It also sets moral standards for how a human being can live, work, create, and contribute. Most importantly, it shows what a human dream can be.

Preparations to Make Human Dreams Come True

If we realize that life is limited and possession is not portable, life becomes dearer. What could be our most beautiful dreams that make life worth its sublime value? Different people may have different dreams, and the same person may have different dreams at different times. No matter what the dreams are, they will benefit greatly from a reality like this:

1) Peace to the World

Humankind has been suffering from continuous wars and killings of innocent people since the dawn of civilization. Once people understand opposites are complementary, brotherhood in the UNUDHR will prevail, which is a herald of peace in the world.

2) No Struggles for Survival

With tremendous successes in science and technology, the production process is being progressively automated beyond imagination every day. Machines are gradually replacing repetitive operations. The world has already produced enough material wealth. It understands that life is limited, possession is not portable, and a possession should be in good use to help humanity. All human beings can enjoy living free from struggles and making a living. Every person who can work should work; everyone should make a unique contribution to the creation of a better world.

People should be able to choose the work they love most that will become a daily source of happiness instead of struggles for survival. The Chinese sage Confucius (551 BC–479 BC) said, "Choose a job you love, and you will never have to work a day in your life."

3) Happiness and Pursuit of Happiness

People will be able to pursue happiness and stop depending on financial situations, including reuniting families and close ones who are torn up by wars or conflicts. They will create new families that are building cells of human societies. Each individual has a family to care for and to be cared for.

4) Education, Research, and Creation

Free from struggling to make a living, people will be able to focus on education, research, and creation to fulfill the love for knowledge and insatiable curiosity that is innate to the human mind. This will liberate the creative potential previously locked up by the daily struggles for survival. According to scientists, human beings are only using 5 percent of their brain capacity and have great potential to achieve miracles in scientific research and art creation.

5) The World Is Not Enough

Scientists predict human beings will hitch their spacecraft to stars in the universe and choose the best of the stars to make their new homes.

Seek the Truth, Do Good, Create Beauty

Realized or not, everyone has a dream that makes life beautiful. Dream means beauty. When our dreams come true, we feel happy; otherwise, we feel disappointed. When we say, "Our dream comes true," we value what is true. When our dreams come true, beauty is integrated with truth.

Our dreams will not come true if we do not work to make them happen. Work here means doing something good for world peace, safety, health, poverty, happiness, education, reproduction, research, and creation. Doing good is the way to make dreams come true. Through the integration of Truth, Goodness, and Beauty, we are becoming one with humanity and the universe. This is also the human brotherhood dream (one for all, all for one) coming true. It is blissful, harmonious happiness that is larger than life.

APPENDIX

UNITED NATIONS UNIVERSAL DECLARATION OF HUMAN RIGHTS

Preamble

Whereas recognition of the inherent dignity and of the equal and inalienable rights of all members of the human family is the foundation of freedom, justice and peace in the world,

Whereas disregard and contempt for human rights have resulted in barbarous acts which have outraged the conscience of mankind, and the advent of a world in which human beings shall enjoy freedom of speech and belief and freedom from fear and want has been proclaimed as the highest aspiration of the common people,

Whereas it is essential, if man is not to be compelled to have recourse, as a last resort, to rebellion against tyranny and oppression, that human rights should be protected by the rule of law,

Whereas it is essential to promote the development of friendly relations between nations,

Whereas the peoples of the United Nations have in the Charter reaffirmed their faith in fundamental human rights, in the dignity and worth of the human person and in the equal rights of men and women and have determined to promote social progress and better standards of life in larger freedom,

Whereas Member States have pledged themselves to achieve, in co-operation with the United Nations, the promotion of universal respect for and observance of human rights and fundamental freedoms,

Whereas a common understanding of these rights and freedoms is of the greatest importance for the full realization of this pledge,

Now, therefore the General Assembly proclaims this Universal Declaration Of Human Rights as a common standard of achievement for all peoples and all nations, to the end that every individual and every organ of society, keeping this Declaration constantly in mind, shall strive by teaching and education to promote respect for these rights and freedoms and by progressive measures, national and international, to secure their universal and effective recognition and observance, both among the peoples of Member States themselves and among the peoples of territories under their jurisdiction.

Article 1.

- All human beings are born free and equal in dignity and rights. They are endowed with reason and conscience and should act towards one another in a spirit of brotherhood.

Article 2.

- Everyone is entitled to all the rights and freedoms set forth in this Declaration, without distinction of any kind, such as race, colour, sex, language, religion, political or other opinion, national or social origin, property, birth or other status. Furthermore, no distinction shall be made on the basis of the political, jurisdictional or international status of the country or territory to which a person belongs, whether it be independent, trust, non-self-governing or under any other limitation of sovereignty.

Article 3.

- Everyone has the right to life, liberty and security of person.

Article 4.

- No one shall be held in slavery or servitude; slavery and the slave trade shall be prohibited in all their forms.

Article 5.

- No one shall be subjected to torture or to cruel, inhuman or degrading treatment or punishment.

Article 6.

- Everyone has the right to recognition everywhere as a person before the law.

Article 7.

- All are equal before the law and are entitled without any discrimination to equal protection of the law. All are entitled to equal protection against any discrimination in violation of this Declaration and against any incitement to such discrimination.

Article 8.

- Everyone has the right to an effective remedy by the competent national tribunals for acts violating the fundamental rights granted him by the constitution or by law.

Article 9.

- No one shall be subjected to arbitrary arrest, detention or exile.

Article 10.

- Everyone is entitled in full equality to a fair and public hearing by an independent and impartial tribunal, in the determination of his rights and obligations and of any criminal charge against him.

Article 11.

- (1) Everyone charged with a penal offence has the right to be presumed innocent until proved guilty according to law in a public trial at which he has had all the guarantees necessary for his defence.
- (2) No one shall be held guilty of any penal offence on account of any act or omission which did not constitute a penal offence, under national or international law, at the time when it was committed. Nor shall a heavier penalty be imposed than the one that was applicable at the time the penal offence was committed.

Article 12.

- No one shall be subjected to arbitrary interference with his privacy, family, home or correspondence, nor to attacks upon his honour and reputation. Everyone has the right to the protection of the law against such interference or attacks.

Article 13.

- (1) Everyone has the right to freedom of movement and residence within the borders of each state.
- (2) Everyone has the right to leave any country, including his own, and to return to his country.

Article 14.

- (1) Everyone has the right to seek and to enjoy in other countries asylum from persecution.
- (2) This right may not be invoked in the case of prosecutions genuinely arising from non-political crimes or from acts contrary to the purposes and principles of the United Nations.

Article 15.

- (1) Everyone has the right to a nationality.
- (2) No one shall be arbitrarily deprived of his nationality nor denied the right to change his nationality.

Article 16.

- (1) Men and women of full age, without any limitation due to race, nationality or religion, have the right to marry and to found a family. They are entitled to equal rights as to marriage, during marriage and at its dissolution.
- (2) Marriage shall be entered into only with the free and full consent of the intending spouses.
- (3) The family is the natural and fundamental group unit of society and is entitled to protection by society and the State.

Article 17.

- (1) Everyone has the right to own property alone as well as in association with others.
- (2) No one shall be arbitrarily deprived of his property.

Article 18.

- Everyone has the right to freedom of thought, conscience and religion; this right includes freedom to change his religion or belief, and freedom, either alone or in community with others and in public or private, to manifest his religion or belief in teaching, practice, worship and observance.

Article 19.

- Everyone has the right to freedom of opinion and expression; this right includes freedom to hold opinions without interference and to seek, receive and impart information and ideas through any media and regardless of frontiers.

Article 20.

- (1) Everyone has the right to freedom of peaceful assembly and association.
- (2) No one may be compelled to belong to an association.

Article 21.

- (1) Everyone has the right to take part in the government of his country, directly or through freely chosen representatives.
- (2) Everyone has the right of equal access to public service in his country.
- (3) The will of the people shall be the basis of the authority of government; this will shall be expressed in periodic and genuine elections which shall be by universal and equal suffrage and shall be held by secret vote or by equivalent free voting procedures.

Article 22.

- Everyone, as a member of society, has the right to social security and is entitled to realization, through national effort and international co-operation and in accordance with the organization and resources of each State, of the economic, social and cultural rights indispensable for his dignity and the free development of his personality.

Article 23.

- (1) Everyone has the right to work, to free choice of employment, to just and favourable conditions of work and to protection against unemployment.
- (2) Everyone, without any discrimination, has the right to equal pay for equal work.
- (3) Everyone who works has the right to just and favourable remuneration ensuring for himself and his family an existence

worthy of human dignity, and supplemented, if necessary, by other means of social protection.

- (4) Everyone has the right to form and to join trade unions for the protection of his interests.

Article 24.

- Everyone has the right to rest and leisure, including reasonable limitation of working hours and periodic holidays with pay.

Article 25.

- (1) Everyone has the right to a standard of living adequate for the health and well-being of himself and of his family, including food, clothing, housing and medical care and necessary social services, and the right to security in the event of unemployment, sickness, disability, widowhood, old age or other lack of livelihood in circumstances beyond his control.
- (2) Motherhood and childhood are entitled to special care and assistance. All children, whether born in or out of wedlock, shall enjoy the same social protection.

Article 26.

- (1) Everyone has the right to education. Education shall be free, at least in the elementary and fundamental stages. Elementary education shall be compulsory. Technical and professional education shall be made generally available and higher education shall be equally accessible to all on the basis of merit.
- (2) Education shall be directed to the full development of the human personality and to the strengthening of respect for human rights and fundamental freedoms. It shall promote understanding, tolerance and friendship among all nations, racial or religious groups, and shall further the activities of the United Nations for the maintenance of peace.

- (3) Parents have a prior right to choose the kind of education that shall be given to their children.

Article 27.

- (1) Everyone has the right freely to participate in the cultural life of the community, to enjoy the arts and to share in scientific advancement and its benefits.
- (2) Everyone has the right to the protection of the moral and material interests resulting from any scientific, literary or artistic production of which he is the author.

Article 28.

- Everyone is entitled to a social and international order in which the rights and freedoms set forth in this Declaration can be fully realized.

Article 29.

- (1) Everyone has duties to the community in which alone the free and full development of his personality is possible.
- (2) In the exercise of his rights and freedoms, everyone shall be subject only to such limitations as are determined by law solely for the purpose of securing due recognition and respect for the rights and freedoms of others and of meeting the just requirements of morality, public order and the general welfare in a democratic society.
- (3) These rights and freedoms may in no case be exercised contrary to the purposes and principles of the United Nations.

Article 30.

- Nothing in this Declaration may be interpreted as implying for any State, group or person any right to engage in any activity or to perform any act aimed at the destruction of any of the rights and freedoms set forth herein.

About the Author

Chauncey Chen is an engineer, a physicist, and an award-winning poet.

He was born in China in 1932. In 1956, as a young assistant professor of physics, he criticized the government and was "reeducated" in a labor camp for more than two years. Later, he became a high school substitute teacher. In the Cultural Revolution (1966–1976), he was sent to the countryside to become a peasant, making about 25 *fens* (about $.05) a day for three years.

In 1978, he was permitted to join his parents and siblings in Hong Kong. He worked as a technical officer in the Hong Kong Public Works Department until he immigrated to the United States as a political refugee in 1981. In the United States, he worked in the New York State Department of Transportation as a technician and as an engineer from 1981 to 2003, when he retired.

In 1999, he published a health book. *Dynamic Chikung* included a project entitled "Complete Democracy in the USA" in which he proposed all authorities in public and private sectors should be periodically and democratically elected to eliminate institutionalized bureaucracy.

Chen lives in New York City. He has a daughter and a son.

www.ingramcontent.com/pod-product-compliance
Lightning Source LLC
Chambersburg PA
CBHW030518290526
45786CB00004B/1514